MEET THE 12 DISCIPLES!

Written By
Anna Aghadiuno

Illustrated By
Gaurav Bhatnagar

This book belongs to

To Babs Stone

MEET THE 12 DISCIPLES!

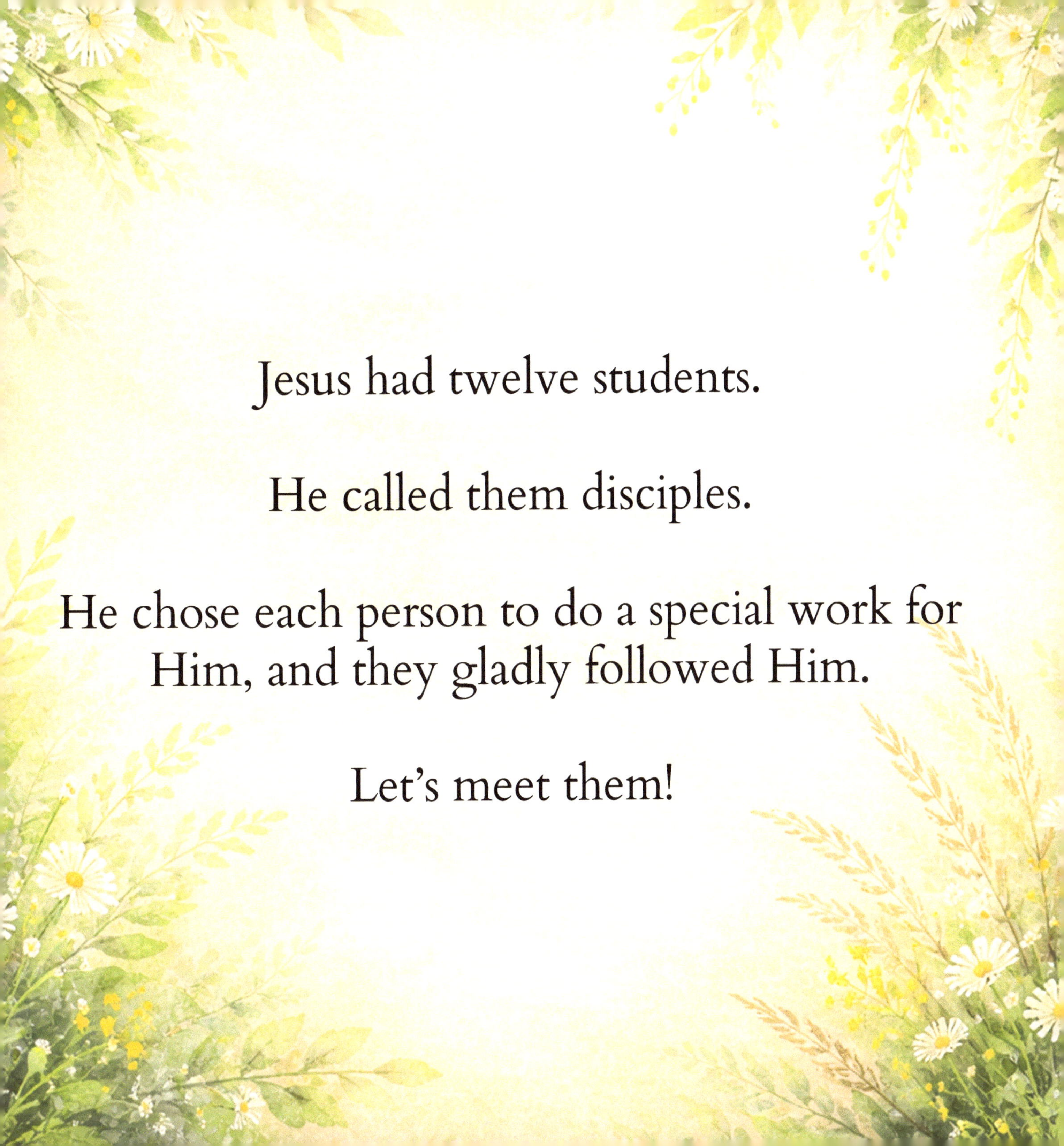

Jesus had twelve students.

He called them disciples.

He chose each person to do a special work for Him, and they gladly followed Him.

Let's meet them!

Hi there!
My name is Peter.

I am a fisherman from Bethsaida. That's a town in Galilee.
My daddy's name is Jonah, and I have a brother named Andrew.
We were both fishermen.

I used to be called Simon, but Jesus called me to follow Him and He changed my name to Peter, which means "THE ROCK".

I love my new name!
Jesus said that I would do a very special work for him.
One day, I denied Jesus three times because I was scared. This made me very sad.
But Jesus forgave me, and I became one of His best students!
I followed Him everywhere He went.

MEET ANDREW!

Hello! My name is Andrew, and I love following Jesus.
I was also a fisherman when Jesus called me.
I have a brother named Peter, and my daddy's name is Jonah.

Jesus and I are very good friends, and I was one of His first disciples.
I was the one who told my brother Peter about Jesus, and he was very
excited!

Jesus told my brother Peter and me to become fishers of men.
We said YES!
One day, we needed food to feed many hungry people, but we had none.
I told Jesus about a little boy who had five loaves of bread and two small fish.

Jesus prayed, and the bread and fish multiplied.
We fed all five thousand people!
WOW! What a miracle!!!

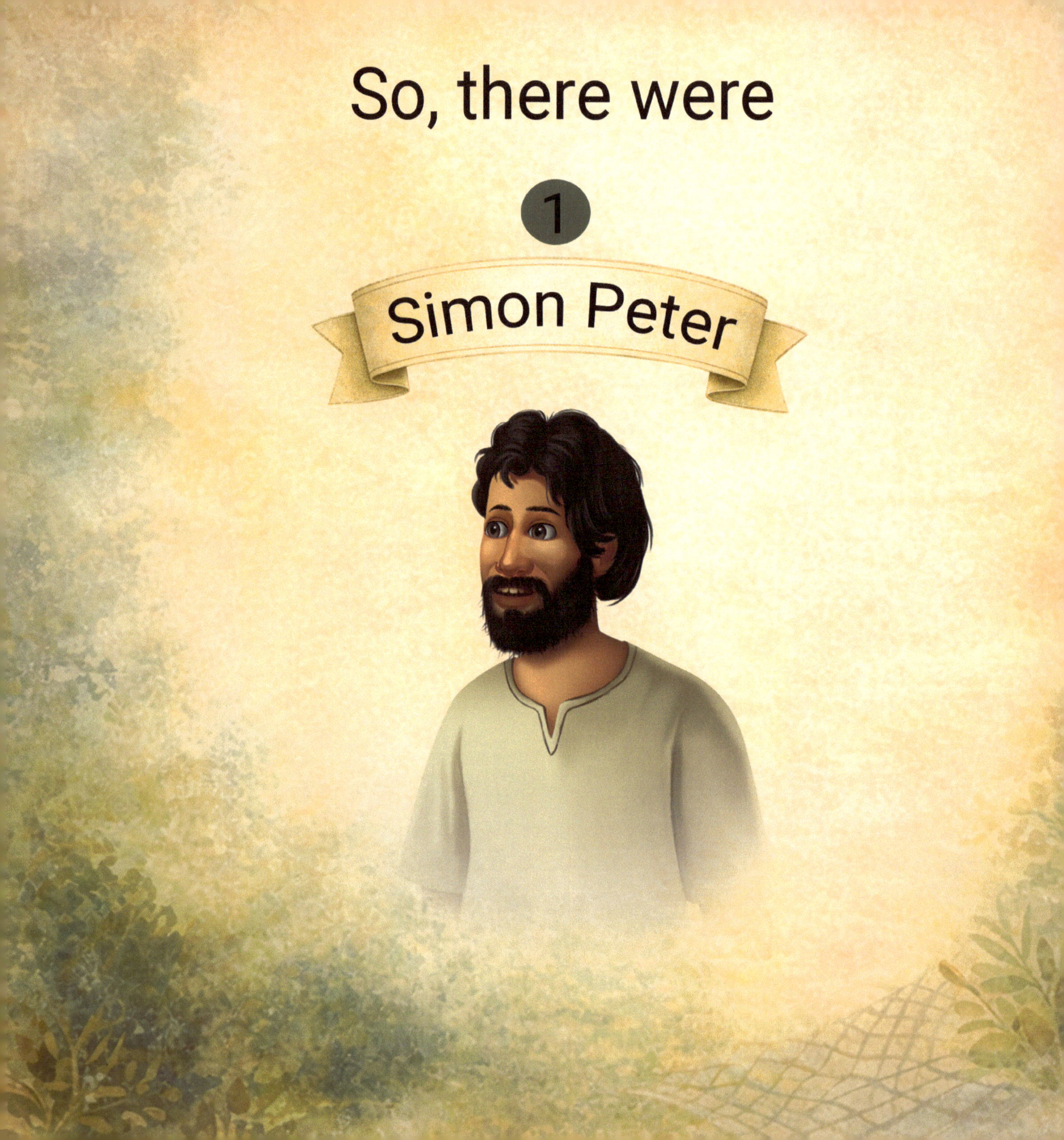
So, there were

1

Simon Peter

2
Andrew

<u>MEET JAMES!</u>

My name is James, and I am happy to be one of Jesus' disciples.
I have a brother named JOHN.
My daddy's name is Zebedee, and my mommy's name is Salome.

I am calm and gentle, but sometimes, I get angry and speak loudly. Jesus is working on my heart, and he called me the "Son of Thunder" That made me laugh!

MEET JOHN!

My name is John.

James is my brother.
James and I were fixing our fishing nets with our dad Zebedee when Jesus called us.

Jesus also called my brother James and me the "Sons of Thunder" because we are resilient and strong!

We are also obedient students, and we followed him everywhere He went.
I love Jesus!

So, there were
1
Simon Peter
2
Andrew

3
James
4
John

MEET PHILIP!

Hi! I'm Philip, and I'm from a place called Bethsaida, in Galilee.

Jesus came to look for me, and when he found me, he said "FOLLOW ME," and so I did!
I am very curious.
That means I always want things explained.

One day, Jesus wanted to feed a crowd of five thousand
People, but we only had five loaves of bread and two small fish!

"That was not enough food!" I said.

But Jesus performed a miracle, and everyone
had plenty to eat!

<u>MEET NATHANIEL!</u>

Hi, my name is Nathaniel, and I'm from a town called Cana, in Galilee
Some people also call me Bartholomew.
My friend, Philip, invited me to come and meet Jesus.

At first, I didn't want to go, but I'm sure glad I did!
Jesus said I am honest and truthful.
I believe Jesus is the Son of God, and I followed him everywhere He went.

So, there were

4
John
5
Philip
6
Nathaniel

MEET THOMAS!

Hi! My name is Thomas, and I love being Jesus's disciple.
I heard that Jesus rose from the dead, but
I doubted it.

Then Jesus appeared to me. He showed me His wounds.

When I saw it, I shouted, "My Lord and my God!"

Then I believed!

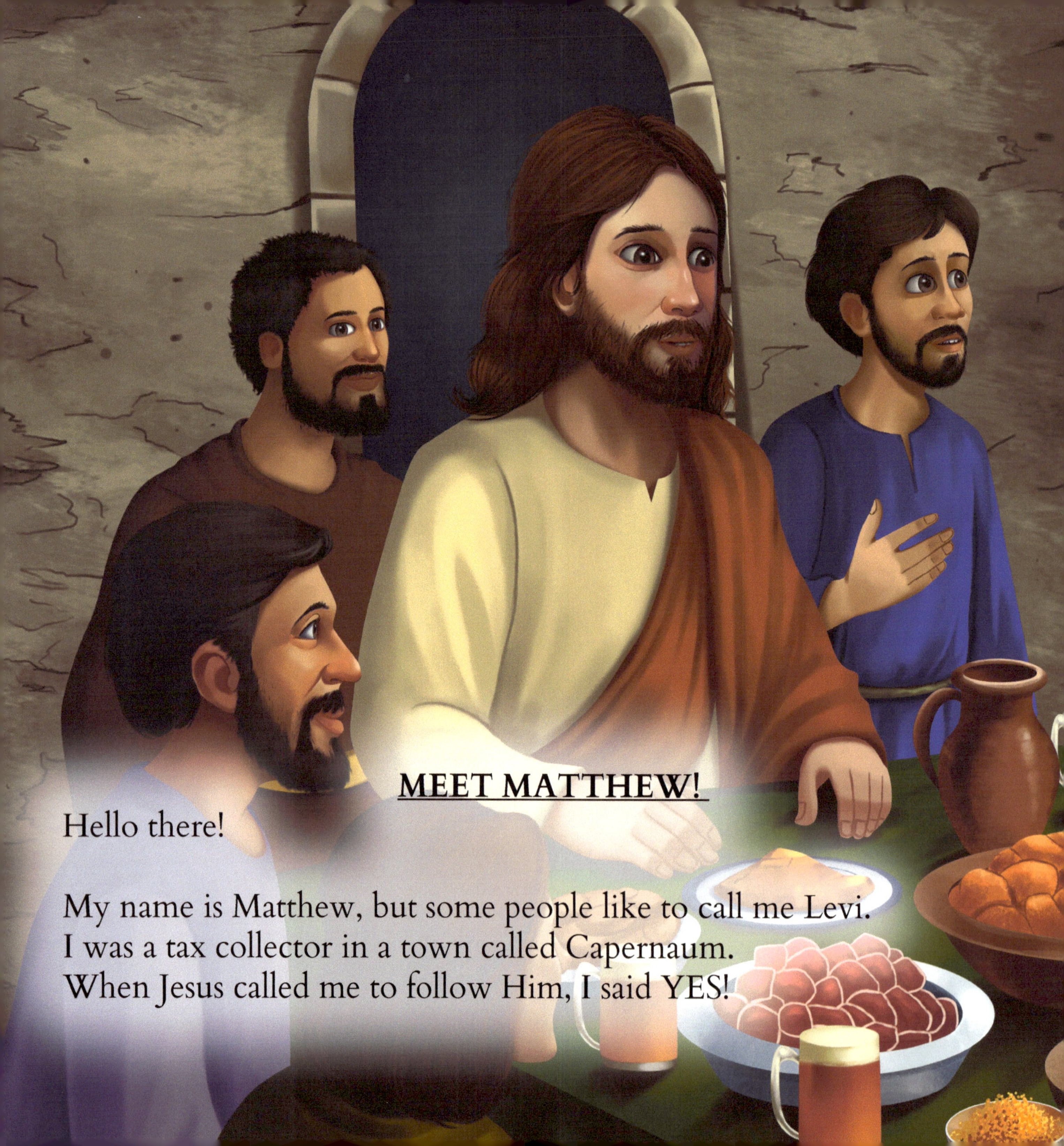

<u>MEET MATTHEW!</u>

Hello there!

My name is Matthew, but some people like to call me Levi.
I was a tax collector in a town called Capernaum.
When Jesus called me to follow Him, I said YES!

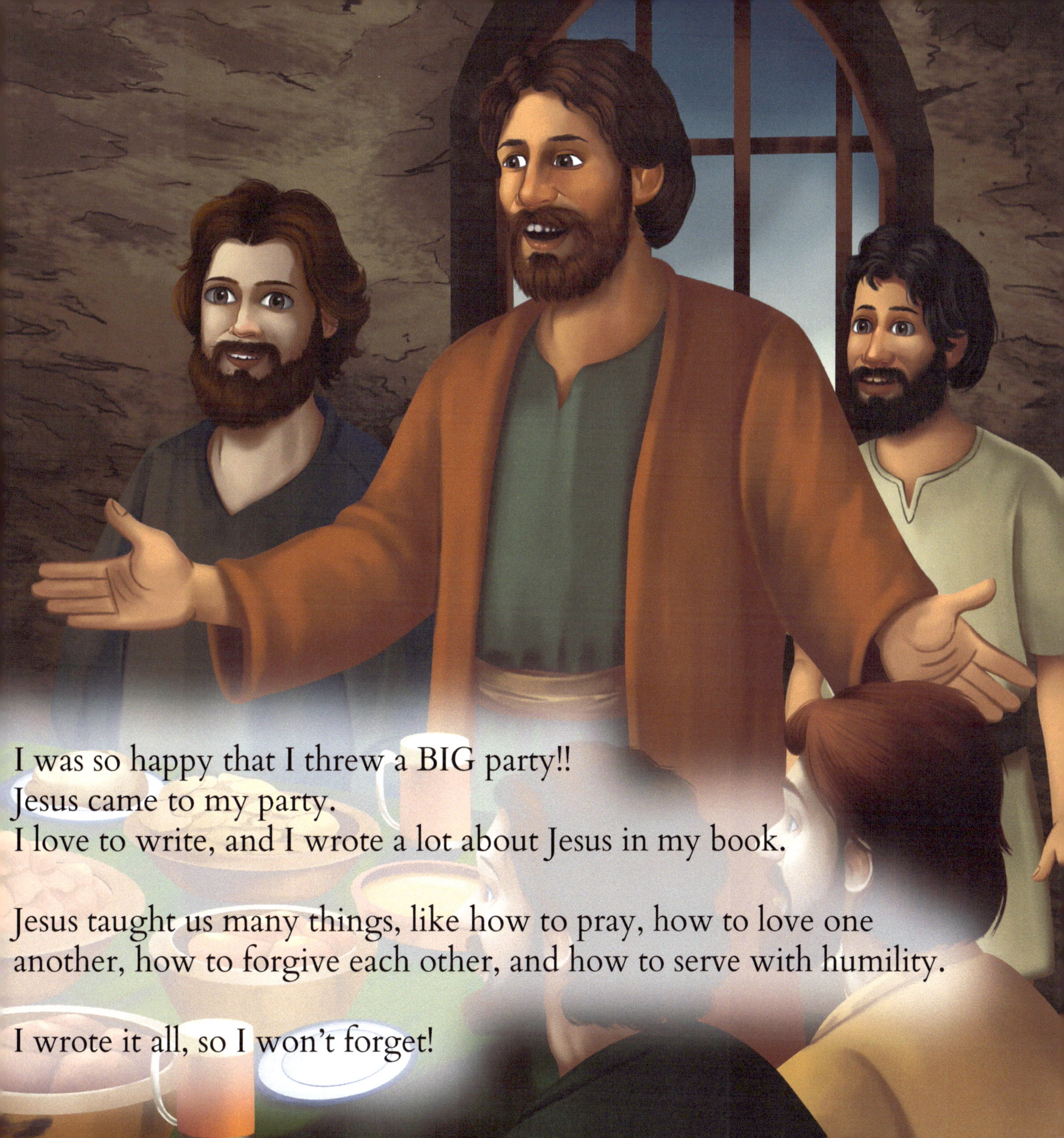

I was so happy that I threw a BIG party!!
Jesus came to my party.
I love to write, and I wrote a lot about Jesus in my book.

Jesus taught us many things, like how to pray, how to love one another, how to forgive each other, and how to serve with humility.

I wrote it all, so I won't forget!

So, there were

5
Philip
6
Nathaniel
7
Thomas
8
Matthew

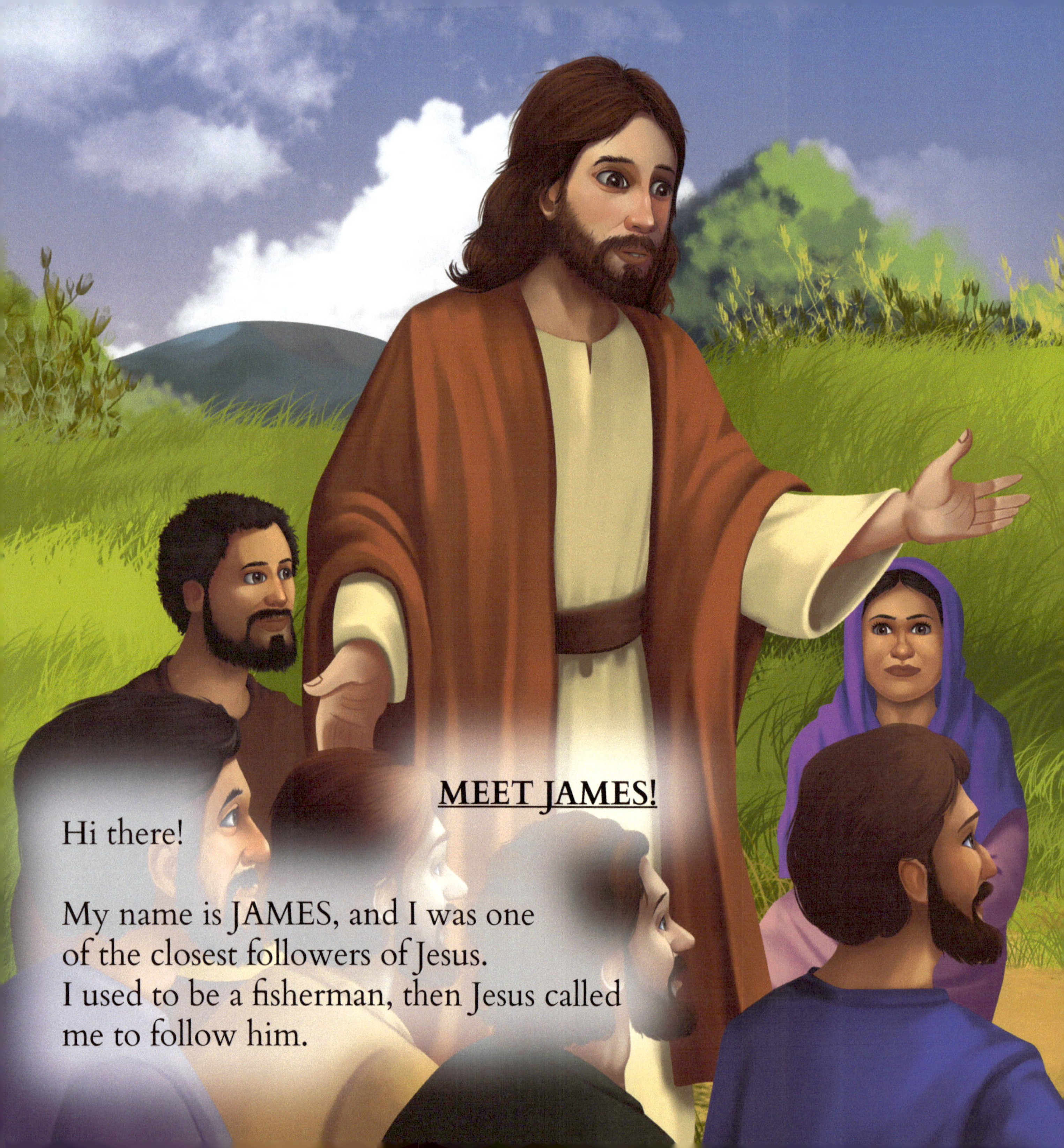
MEET JAMES!

Hi there!

My name is JAMES, and I was one
of the closest followers of Jesus.
I used to be a fisherman, then Jesus called
me to follow him.

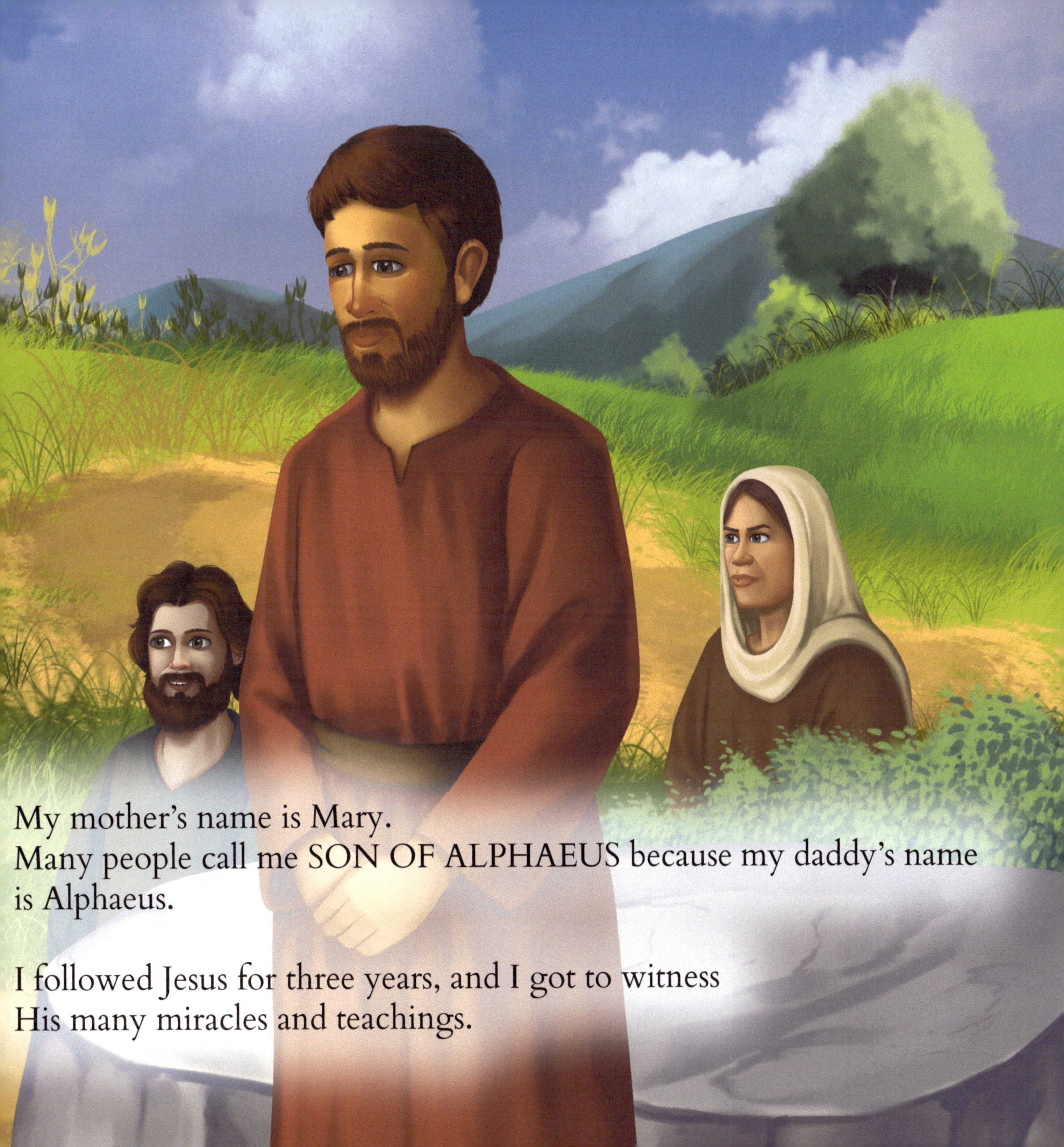

My mother's name is Mary.
Many people call me SON OF ALPHAEUS because my daddy's name
is Alphaeus.

I followed Jesus for three years, and I got to witness
His many miracles and teachings.

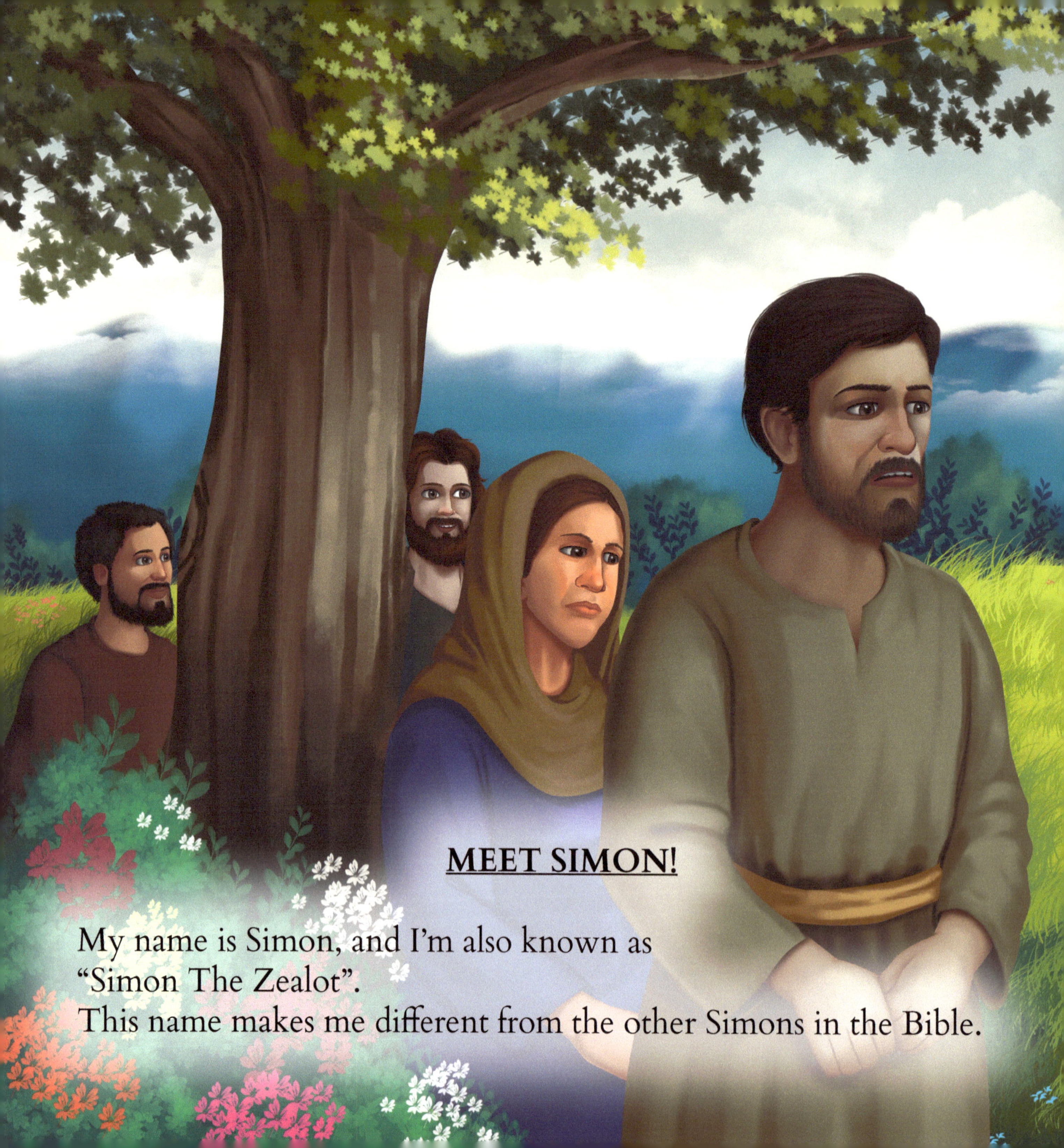

<u>**MEET SIMON!**</u>

My name is Simon, and I'm also known as
"Simon The Zealot".
This name makes me different from the other Simons in the Bible.

I heard Jesus preaching, and I saw many of His miracles.

I was a devoted follower of Jesus and one of His closest friends!

So, there were

6
Nathaniel
7
Thomas
8
Matthew
9
James
10
Simon

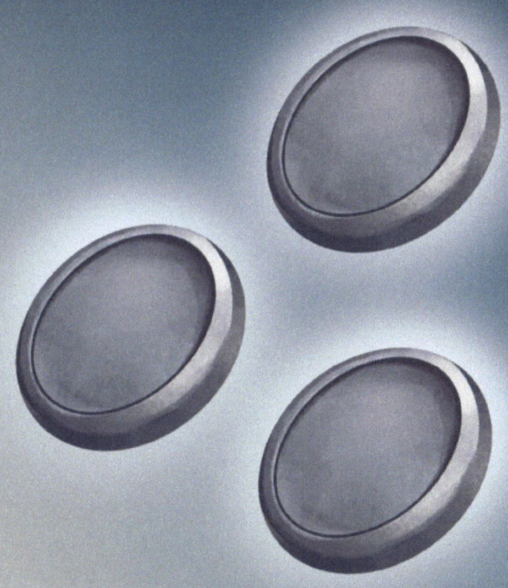

<u>MEET JUDAS!</u>

Hi! My name is Judas.
Jesus called me to help him build His ministry, and I agreed!

I oversaw keeping all the money for the other disciples,
So, that made me a TREASURER.
I betrayed Jesus for 30 pieces of silver, and then I felt bad afterwards.

<u>MEET THADDEUS!</u>

Hello! My name is Thaddeus.
Some people also call me JUDE.

Jesus called me to be one of His twelve disciples who would proclaim
the Kingdom of Heaven.

I believed Jesus, so I agreed!

I continued to talk about Jesus throughout my life, and I focused on His ministry.

So, there were

7
Thomas
8
Matthew
9
James
10
Simon
11
Judas
12
Thaddeus

Who is your favorite disciple?

About the Author

Ms. Anna is a devoted follower of the Lord with a heartfelt desire to bring Bible stories into the hearts of children all over the world. She has a deep passion for nurturing, teaching, and inspiring children, and her love for them shines through everything she does.

Anna is the proud mother of two grown children and is lovingly called "Mom" by many more whose lives she has touched along the way. Her lifelong commitment to children led her to found a non-profit organization dedicated to meeting the needs of children, as well as an elementary school in Nigeria, where she continues to make a lasting impact.

Currently living in Atlanta, Georgia, USA, Anna writes with the hope that every child who reads her books will feel loved, valued, and drawn closer to God through timeless Bible stories shared in a warm and joyful way.